such small hands

Printed in the United States of America
Published in 2020 by Dog's Heart Press

ISBN 978-1-935716-46-4

Cover photo by Ryan Walton

such small hands
An Anti-Aversives Primer

rain jordan

Dog's Heart Press

nothing which we are to perceive in this world
equals the power of your intense fragility . . .
the voice of your eyes is deeper than all roses.
nobody, not even the rain, has such small hands.

-ee cummings

CONTENTS

Introduction

When it comes to aversives in dog handling, many positive reinforcement proponents recommend that we focus on ourselves and our own work rather than trying to change those who use aversives. The problem with that is, even if each of us is a universe, we are very small ones. We may do stellar work with those who come to us, but what about everyone else? Those caught inside the universes of pain, force, and fear are not helped by our parallel universes no matter how positive. The long-standing constellations of harm that make up a large part of our history with companion animals give cover. These constellations blanket us with a misleading sense that it's all beautiful in the grand scheme.

Edison said "I have not reached my conclusions through study of traditions; I have reached them through the study of hard fact .... What we need is search for fundamentals, not reiteration of traditions born in days when [we] knew even less than we do now." A proponent of kindness, Scully says, "Sometimes tradition and habit are just that—

comfortable excuses to leave things be, even when they are unjust and unworthy."

Modern science provides plenty of evidence that aversives result in lasting harm. Those of us who are certified in animal behavior and training have an obligation to educate against harm. From my perspective, we cannot provide an education in well-being if we refuse to discuss one of the components of the core curriculum. For us, looking at the history of aversives and working to stop history from repeating itself over and over in the universe of each of our companions is a moral imperative.

Buckminster Fuller is known for his belief that change comes not from fighting existing reality, but from building a new model that makes the existing model obsolete; however, he was *best* known for the creation of dome homes, a model that did not change existing reality but instead became quickly obsolete itself. Let's not let that happen to anti-aversive dog training.

Mandela knew that education is the vehicle that drives change. Mead instructs us to "never doubt that a small group of thoughtful, committed citizens can change the world." Whether the following are in fact Mother Teresa's words or a paraphrase of them, "I alone cannot change the world, but I can cast a stone across the waters to create many ripples" is at once reminiscent of the glass houses proverb and a piece of complementary wisdom.

The goal of this book isn't to throw stones. It is an invitation to begin skipping the stones that create the ripples of change.

-Rain Jordan

A Note about Terms

In this text I sometimes use the word "reward" when referring to the high value food reinforcers used in R+ (positive reinforcement) training. I also use "handler" interchangeably with "owner" and "trainer." The term "handler" in this text is to be understood as any person interacting with or acting on the animal.

An aversive is any stimulus a dog seeks to avoid or escape. This includes any person, place, thing, or experience that the dog would prefer to avoid, whether or not avoidance is demonstrated. A simple way of thinking about it: if the dog does not like it, it is aversive for that dog.

Many things that some dog owners do habitually, albeit unwittingly in many cases, are aversive; sternly scolding, commanding or yelling No, yelling in general, squirting with water, pulling on a collar or leash, and so on. Additionally, many common dog service providers to whom we consider taking our dogs may be aversive to our dogs. Even we and our affection can be aversive; if your dog does not like being hugged (most dogs don't), then hugging is an aversive for your dog.

That said, I want to be clear: With a few exceptions, the dog decides what is aversive.

The exceptions include things such as pain, force, intimidation, coercion, startle, and fear-leveraging. These are inherently aversive.

It is interesting to note that some people have

assigned the euphemism "getting their attention" to the aversive action known as startling the dog even though startling the dog is a form of fear-leveraging and/or intimidation. If you want attention from your dog that leads to a happy result, do something nice, not something startling.

Many shock collar users claim that the "vibration" setting of shock collars are not aversive but rather merely "get their attention." And yet a well-known shock trainer recently stated, regarding the various settings of a shock collar, that "I've seen dogs piss themselves on vibration."

A common but inaccurate claim made regarding the purposeful aversive known as a shock collar—euphemistically, misleadingly called a "remote communication collar," "stim," "tens unit," "vibration collar" and various other verbal fabrications— on dogs is that their dog doesn't mind it, or gets excited when it comes out, and therefore, it isn't aversive. For example: A shock collar user claimed that the collar is not aversive to her individual dog—that in fact, when the dog sees the collar, the user claims, the dog becomes happy because it means he is about to be let out to explore or play on the user's acreage.

The shock collar user does not understand that the secondary conditioning—that is, the positive association developed to getting to go outside and explore once the collar is put on— is simply overshadowing the aversive nature of the shock collar. The dog's past experiences of an uncomfortable stimulus—being shocked or threatened by the potential of the collar—are overshadowed by the dog's anticipation of a stimulus he enjoys and strongly desires—the acreage.

Being happy about the opportunity to explore does not mean the dog doesn't find the collar aversive. The dog may suppress his fear in order to obtain what he most *wants*: access to outside. Just as Pavlov's dogs' salivation at the sound of the bell does not mean that the dogs enjoy the bell, but rather that they enjoy what comes after the bell, the dog is not happy because of the collar; he is happy because the appearance of the device, in his experience, predicts going outside. This does not mean the dog doesn't suffer pain, fear, or discomfort from the shock collar. It only means that the dog values going outside more than he dislikes the collar.

Sometimes dogs avoid an aversive by behaving in ways considered acceptable by a human's demands. A dog who has had a shoe thrown at him for barking may stop barking when he sees a human lift a shoe. In such ways, aversives may "work" to suppress behaviors temporarily. The temporary nature of aversives' efficacy is demonstrated by the fact that a dog eventually, or soon, barks again even though the aversive stopped a previous bark. Aversives are not cures and should not be considered lasting solutions.

It's important to note that for some dogs, such as extremely fearful dogs, simply having a human be or move in their presence can be aversive. Thus, in some cases, what a dog decides is aversive might be something *we* think is harmless or minute. In the care of companion animals, nothing is so minute that it should be undeserving of mindful reconsideration.

We love our dogs and therefore if they are unhappy, we cannot help but unhappy. It should be self-evident that an anti-aversives lifestyle increases happiness for our animals and for us.

The risks of suppressing behavior via use of aversives include:

The need to escalate the intensity or frequency, or both, of that aversive over time in order to achieve the same result. A dog who is "misbehaving" is usually doing so as a result of an underlying emotion, association, need, or condition in need of treatment. Because undesired behavior is fueled by these underlying conditions, a dog who is receiving aversive treatment as attempts to modify the undesired behavior eventually will tend to escalate rather than recover from the undesired behavior—in a more fervent effort to gain whatever it is he needs. Sadly, instead of obtaining help, a dog living with physical or emotional suffering who also lives with a user of aversives will only get more suffering in response to his plea for help. Therefore, the aversive becomes increasingly more cruel and dangerous. When the undesired behavior returns, a shoe thrower may decide to throw more shoes, more often, or larger, heavier shoes or other items, or throw them harder. An occasional brief squirt with water eventually isn't enough to suppress the undesired behavior—after all, *it does nothing to address the need that underlies the undesired behavior—so a more frequent squirt may come next, then perhaps a soaking; when that no longer works, a user might decide to add a second aversive. Now the dog is getting soaked, plus getting yelled at, or threatened, etc. It is cruel to respond with pain, intimidation, force, or scare tactics to a dog who is asking for our help. This type of cruelty is often dangerous as well, for both the dog and humans.

An increase or addition of negative feelings & associations related to the aversive itself, but also related to the deliverer of the aversive, to those similar to the deliverer, and potentially to any other stimuli present at the time the aversive is delivered.

Since undesired behavior is typically a manifestation of negative feelings or associations, responding with an aversive—a stimulus that creates negative feelings and associations—will result eventually in **an increase of undesired behavior, or of additional undesired behaviors**, correlative to new negative associations having been formed via use of the original aversive.

The American Animal Hospital Association states in its Canine and Feline Behavior Management Guidelines that "aversive training causes behavior problems in normal animals and hastens progression of behavioral disorders in distressed animals," adding that aversive techniques "often suppress signals of impending aggression, rendering any aggressive dog more dangerous."

Increased risk of injury and/or euthanasia. Studies have correlated the use of aversives with anywhere from a 25% to a 40% increase in the likelihood of undesired behavior, including increased aggression, as well as new aggression in previously non-aggressive dogs. Since behavior problems are one of the main reasons for elective euthanasia, aversives are thereby correlated with euthanasia. Sadly, the top reason for elective euthanasia of dogs 3 years old and under is undesired behavior. An anti-aversives lifestyle can contribute significantly to changing that.

---

*Unless the dog is executing the undesired behavior in order to access a basic need, such as attention. In that case as well, even the negative attention garnered will result in an increase in the undesired behavior, since behavior that is reinforced will continue or increase. 23

What does "Anti-Aversives" Mean?

Anti-Aversives is a term I use to describe a person or practice who—while acknowledging that some aversives, such as thunderstorms and other naturally occurring phenomena, are out of human control—is adamantly against the leveraging and purposeful use of aversives.

An Anti-Aversives trainer rejects the purposeful use of aversives such as shock collars, squirting, scolding, fear-leveraging, et cetera.

An Anti-Aversives trainer also goes to great lengths to avoid a dog's exposure to aversives—not only those within the trainer's control, but also to those outside of the trainer's direct control, including nature-caused and human-caused, whether purposeful or inadvertent. Fireworks, for example, are aversive to many dogs. Therefore someone who is anti-aversive and is caring for a dog would probably not use fireworks, would not expose a dog to fireworks, and would do whatever possible to protect the dog from inadvertent exposure to fireworks, including long-distance auditory or visual exposure. Some people create temporary bunkers in the center of their home and farthest away from the fireworks-related stimuli as possible. Others take their dogs for holidays to towns like Carmel-by-the-Sea, where fireworks are outlawed and the law is vigorously enforced. An example of avoiding nature-caused aversives might be choosing not to live where thunderstorms are common.

Being anti-aversive does not mean you will never panic and pull on a leash or raise your voice; you're only human and if your dog darts out in the middle of a busy street with a car headed straight for her, pulling on the leash to save her life would likely be an involuntary if not reasonable response, and yelling might be an understandable natural panic response in such a situation. Being anti-aversive means being a human who is against the use of aversives on animals, who also does everything possible to avoid inadvertent aversives.

A Brief History of Animals and Aversives

Around 125 B.C., a Roman farmer named Marcos Varro began recording details about his herding dog training practices. In 55 B.C., Roman armies brought their trained dogs with them to invade the British countryside. While I can't prove this, I think it's reasonable to say that aversives were probably part of their training practices.

In Germany around 1914, Konrad Most, a police dog trainer, was hired to train military dogs. Thereafter he opened a training center for assistance dogs and other working dogs. He advocated the use of aversives including "compulsive inducements such as the switch, the spiked collar, and forced compliance"; his principles are still used today in police and military settings.

In the USA, dog training took hold in the 1700s, mainly for use with sporting dogs. In the 1920s, boarding kennels offered dog training to pet dog owners. Then in 1933, two women, Helen Whitehouse Walker and Blanche Saunders, began their road trip to promote dog training, and it appears that by 1934 the AKC had jumped on, or least side-car-d, the bandwagon. Unfortunately, as is demonstrated in the video discussed below, the Whitehouse-Saunders wagon was a vehicle bearing not happy tots or toys, but torment for dogs.

A promotional video from 1954 featuring Saunders' methods appears currently on YouTube. As I'm viewing it, the first aversive occurrence I note is a clip of a little girl strangle-cuddling a small, white, curly haired dog—the dog appears stressed and since it's fair to assume the dog would prefer not to be strangle-cuddled, here is where the first aversive appears in the video. Next up is a clip from a dog show; the dogs are lined up for the judge, who grasps and lifts a dog by the sides of the neck, about a foot off the ground. This is followed by a woman patting her show dog hard enough that the dog is taken off his front feet by it. (It is very possible she was unaware of that.) Next the narrator introduces the schools where dogs may "learn the good manners that every pet should know"; these are depicted by a circling parade of dogs on leashes, with handlers performing leash tugs. There's also, next, a literal parade of dogs, complete with a two-dog spat and leash jerk response by handler. Then things get a bit more disturbing. The narrator states "the little balls of fur turn into such nightmares"; the declaration is followed by a young man flat-palm hitting a dog who runs around a living room chair to get away from the young man's aversive behavior. The dog hides and cowers behind the chair and the young man hits him again. Next, in the housetraining section, a boy discovers his dog eliminating indoors so grabs the dog's collar and harshly yanks and drags the dog around, then points to the spot. The dog is clearly afraid, and the boy then chokes up on the collar, holds it tight, and spanks the dog several times on the side of her shoulder. The video continues with more dogs dragged by their leashes, being shoved while tethering, and one young dog—whose journey from puppy to juvenile we witness—having her throat skin pinched and used in place of a collar for whipping her around as punishment for crying when left alone, followed by several hard smacks on the face and head as the pup tries to escape, followed by more smacking on the head and face for barking when she hears the owner has returned home from a brief trial against separation anxiety. Viewers are then taken through this same dog's development as she grows older; as her "training" continues, she is punished for lying on a chair, by the owner picking her up by the skin of her back and neck, then tossing her to the floor. Next, the narrator describes as we watch that owner place a set mouse trap on that chair, and then footage of the clearly distressed pup, stress panting, lying on the floor in front of that same chair.

This poor dog is also kneed in the chest for jumping up to greet her owner, then entrapped with a plate of food purposely left as bait on a coffee table and hit hard on the face and head for accepting the invitation to go for the bait, and then has rocks thrown at her after accepting another invitation to chase a car. It is of interest to note that at this point, the topic changes and the narrator presents that now the dog is older and "understands" and is a happy and friendly dog. Yet the film appears to have switched out the dog for a different older dog for this section—a lookalike, but not likely the same dog. After a moment of narration claiming how great the dog's life is, more and harder leash jerks begin, followed by a physically forced "sit" and "down," followed by more leash jerks when the dog doesn't instantly come to the owner when commanded to do so. Still more dogs are hit, dragged, and generally traumatized, while the narrator tells us that most dogs can take a "good old-fashioned spanking." We are told that a dog refusing dinner must be sick and so are shown a little boy repeatedly attempt a forced rectal temperature-taking on the dog. The "sick" dog presents with a tail tucked tightly up against her torso, ears pinned back, repeatedly turning away from the boy, and cowering. The dog likely *is* sick—of living a life filled with aversives.

Near the end of this video comes a plea from the narrator, who has taken the voice of the dogs, to "help us feel safe." This irony would be laughable if it weren't so devastating to dogs *and* humans.

The text description of the video includes this at the end: "Blanche Saunders worked for the American Kennel Club and produced many of their dog obedience training methods. Blanche Saunders also was a dog trainer for the ASPCA." The ingraining of aversives use on our pets threads even through unexpected places.

Given this history of acts and attitudes, is it any wonder that aversives seem as if coded in the humane genome? As we know, however, genetics and epigenetic components to behavior do not prohibit change. They simply make it more difficult, which means we have to work harder at it. We must develop a devotion to becoming an anti-aversives culture.

Somewhere between the 1930s and the 1950s, Marian Breland Bailey was key in developing and promoting science-backed, humane training. She was a student of B. F. Skinner, and she eventually married the renowned trainer Bob Bailey. Together they pioneered the use of the clicker as a conditioned reinforcer for animals in training.

After WWII came aversives proponent William Koehler, who expressed adamant disdain of food use and psychology in animal training. Koehler was first a war dog trainer, and then a trainer for many breed clubs as well as for Walt Disney studios. Koehler's 1962 book on dog training was the inspiration for multiple court cases, and was banned in Arizona for a while.

Shock collars entered the scene in the 1960s, where they were initially used on hunting dogs. In 1980, the Center for Veterinary Medicine, which is a branch of the FDA, stated that complaints about shock collars were corroborated by FDA testing, that harm included "severe burns in the collar area and possible personality adjustment injuries to the dogs," and that the shocking mechanism was "activated not only by barking but by vehicle horns, slamming doors, or any other loud noise. CVM concurred in regulatory action against the device since it was deemed to be dangerous to the health of the animal."

It wasn't until the 1980s that less aversive, more positive methods rose, thanks to training pros including Karen Pryor and Ian Dunbar. Today, positive methods are still trying to undo the damage a culture of pain, force, intimidation, and fear has done to dogs, and trying to prevent further damage, by encouraging the public to replace aversives with R+ and anti-aversives classical conditioning.

While positive trainers and aversives trainers remain at odds and rhetoric can escalate on both sides, advocates of aversives seem more willing to go on the offensive, whereas positive trainers as a culture prefer not to engage with aversives trainers in aversive ways. Although avoiding aversives like verbal wars is honorable, in these situations, that avoidance tends to result in the spread of aversives due to successful persuasion of the public by aversives proponents, since the loudest voices in the room are the ones to be heard.

You can't fight fire with soft breaths. You don't fight fire with tears.

Aristotle was one of the first to perform experiments on live animals, and while we may infer, we do not know how he and others treated animals outside of the laboratory setting. We do know that many experiments since then, including those of Pasteur (induction of anthrax in sheep), Pavlov (canine digestive system manipulation, restraint & shock, et cetera), and Seligman (restraint and force, in the form of the Pavlovian Hammock, & shock) to name just a few. The first animals were shot into space in the 1940s and most recently in 2018.

The first court trial, prosecution, and execution as capital punishment of an animal—a pig—appears to have been in 1266 in France. Also tried and frequently sentenced to execution were bulls, cows, horses, dogs, sheep, mules, rats, eels, dolphins, and an egg-laying rooster, among others. Putting animals on trial in Europe continued through the 18th century. Given this history, it shouldn't be too surprising that Jean Donaldson describes euthanasia of (most) biting dogs as execution.

In the winter of 1866, Henry Bergh presented his thoughts and hopes for the welfare of animals to a room of people, including the mayor, in New York, after which 100 of those people signed his Declaration for the Rights of Animals, pledging to fight against cruelty to animals. This had been the first animal protection lecture ever delivered in the USA.

Next, Bergh founded the ASPCA, and nine days later, the state passed a law prohibiting cruelty to animals, with Bergh and his ASPCA as the law's enforcer.

The first beneficiaries of Bergh's charter were working draft horses, who had commonly suffered beatings, illness, deprivation, and extreme overwork. While the public scoffed, calling his mission ridiculous, he persisted, facilitating the arrest and prosecutions of abusive horse drivers, improving protections for the horses, and fighting for improvements to the handling of dogs and against abuses of them, "particularly at the hands of city dogcatchers." Dogs were being rounded up from the streets, their yards, and even from their owner's arms. Because the pound paid 50 cents per dog to anyone turning in a dog, teenage boys would steal people's pet dogs for profit.

Every day each summer, the pound would kill all dogs not quickly reclaimed. The killings were public spectacles in which "as many as 80 dogs at a time were drowned, with the largest dogs beaten on the head with a club until they stayed underwater." (It's important to mention that records show many days in which more than 200 or 300 dogs were drowned per day.) The dogs were placed together in an iron cage and dunked repeatedly into the East River until all had drowned—an emotional and behavioral cacophony satisfying the human passion for results over process, and highlighting human indifference to the emotional and physical suffering of animals.

Advocating for dogs and against the city's

policies regarding them, Bergh improved the conditions for dogs at the pound, began paying the fees leveraged upon the poor who wanted their dogs back from the pound, enacted a law prohibiting the pound from accepting dogs from teenage boys, and prosecuted dog catchers for animal cruelty, which resulted in an 80% reduction in dog killings.

Bergh had expressed a desire to abolish the pound; the city, tired of fighting him, offered to pay his ASPCA instead to run it. He refused, declaring that doing so would support the torture of dogs.

Thanks to Bergh's work, by the end of 1910, almost every major city in the nation had opened an animal protection organization modeled after his.

Henry Bergh devoted the last twenty-some years of his life to actively working for the welfare of animals. During this time, he had expressed concern about what might become of the ASPCA after he was gone, and after his death in 1888 his fears became reality: Against Bergh's wishes, the ASPCA traded its animal advocacy & protection charter for a contract to run the city pound, and soon became "New York City's leading killer of dogs.... By the early 1900s, hundreds of thousands of dogs and cats had lost their lives to the ASPCA, and in cities across the country, SPCAs and humane societies followed suit."

Mr. Bergh, it was a stalwart effort.

Dear readers, it's time to complete the mission.

In a pet culture such as ours, dogs are expected to live by our human rules and mores, in several tiers: first by the rules of the country, then by the rules of the state, then by the rules of the city, then sometimes, by the rules of a landlord or homeowner's association, and then, on top of all that, by whatever idiosyncratic rules each dog's owner—and often, family, friends, and associates—further assigns. Since dogs are unable, so far as we know, to wholly understand our lanugage, at this point I'm tempted to posit that the situation of dogs trying to live by our pile of human-oriented rules is itself an aversive situation, or at least a strong set up for one.

I am not saying I'm against having pets, so don't jump. After all, literally millions of at-risk dogs, cats, and other animals need good people—anti-aversives people—to help them survive in the animal-aversive world and care properly for them. Instead, I seek to transform our pet culture to an anti-aversives culture, for the sake of pets everywhere, as well as for the sake of those who love them. Before that can happen, the culture must achieve increased self-honesty—what we more diplomatically call "awareness."

Compared to other cultures, our relative freedom and prosperity mean that we can give our dogs anything we wish, and that we can do as we please in general. Might this also feed our feeling of entitlement to use aversives? If so, isn't it possible, with a little extra effort, to have freedom and prosperity *and* kindness toward animals?

Following are examples of experiences that dogs living in a household-pet culture would likely experience as aversive. These are not all-inclusive lists but instead are representative groupings. You'll note that many of the listed aversives occur inadvertently. People don't all, or always, feel entitled regarding their dogs.

Examples of Aversive Conditions that Household Pet Dogs Experience or may have Experienced:

Living in puppy mills
Living with noise or pollution
Living outdoors

Living mostly alone
Living confined
Living with nothing to do
Living chained/tethered
Living with insufficient exercise
Living with threatening animals
Living with poor nutrition
Living with threatening people
Living without health care
Living in hazard-filled homes
Living with those who harm them
Inescapable exposure to loud, angry, volatile, violent, unpredictable, uncontrollable, overreactive, or cynophobic people.

Examples of Things in Our Culture that are or can be Aversive to Pet Dogs:

Shock Collars
Prong Collars
Choke Chains
Bark Collars
Slip Leads
Catch Poles

Martingale Collars
Scolding
Shake Cans
Spray Bottles
Airhorns
Cages
Crates
Kennels
Electric Fences
Transports
Vans
Trucks
Cars
Hats
Sunglasses
Door Slams
Hoses
Brooms
Mops
Vacuum Cleaners
Shelters
Shelter Workers
Rescuers
Change of Homes

Training

Grooming

Boarding

Veterinary Experiences

Family & Friends

People Arguing

Awkwardly-Moving People

People Yelling

People in General

Other Pets

Bathtubs/Bathing

Fireworks

Guns

Traffic

Vehicle Backfires

Motorcyles

Bicycles

Skateboards

Alpha Rolls

Helicoptering

Hunger

Cold

Heat

Holiday Gatherings

Holiday Environment Changes
Leash Walks
Leash Pulls
Leash Yanks
Leash Corrections
Any Corrections
Being Yelled At
Being Picked Up
Being Held
Being Held Down
Being Handled
New Places
New People
New Anything
Feeling Exposed
Feeling Helpless
Feeling Threatened or in Danger
Not Being Allowed to Run and Hide
Not Being Allowed to Express Discomfort
Not Being Allowed to Say I'm Scared
Not Being Allowed to Say No

Examples of Common Aversive Experiences
Household Pet Dogs Have with Humans:

Finger Pointing in Face
Nagging
Body-Grabbing
Collar Grabs
Muzzle Grabs
Tail Grabs
Ear Grabs
Scruffing
Nose-Bopping
Flank-Smacking
Forced Grooming
Forced Nail Trims
Forced Veterinary Procedures
Unwelcome Hands Invading Face / Head / Feet / Body / Belly

Considering our dogs' myriad aversive experiences throughout their lives, it is not much of a stretch to posit that they have been marginalized.

This conclusion is further bolstered by the fact that our household pet dogs represent only about 17 to 23 percent of all dogs. The reality is that across the world, about 80% of dogs do not live as household pets. Instead, they live as free-roaming dogs, either "owned"—which means fed and loved by an individual or a community but not kept in a home, structure, or yard—or free-roaming feral dogs. Behavioral soundness seems to be a common trait of free-roaming dogs. That behavioral soundness would change drastically if shock collars and other purposeful aversives were introduced into their populations. Imagine the shock and harm to those creatures if their numbers were invaded by crates, collars, and unruly hands delivering a vast collection of aversives.

We cannot arbitrarily change the rules of safety on our dogs, however; they are accustomed to their lifestyles, whether happy or elsewise. Any helpful change would need to be methodically implemented over generations and contextually sound. Making our pet dogs free-roaming isn't a viable possibility for most of our contexts, nor would our dogs adapt well. Not only would this sort of change take many small steps over generations, but it would be immediately and over the long term unsafe in our high vehicle traffic contexts.

Nevertheless, thinking about how the 80%

live may help us rethink how we set up life for our 20%.

There are in essence three categories of stimuli that have a strong potential of being aversive to dogs: Non-controllable, Semi-controllable, and Controllable. Within these are subcategories, as described below:

NON-CONTROLLABLE:

Aversives outside of a handler's control are generally natural phenomena, such as thunder, lightning, and other weather or natural disasters. Potential non-nature-born aversives outside of a handler's control would include things like power outages, accidental explosions, et cetera.

SEMI-CONTROLLABLE

Examples of aversives within a handler's indirect or partial control may include things like overcrowded or overstimulating situations—e.g., heavy vehicle or foot traffic in the handler's chosen neighborhood, or deciding to take a dog to a festival or other high traffic area—,electronic or other household noises, disliked people, disliked animals, and violent and other harmful or fear-inducing behaviors between humans in the household, perfumes and other odors, and so on. These are in the semi-controllable category because they can be at least partially avoided or addressed by our choices: where to live, what equipment to buy or use, who to spend time with or live with, what we wear, et cetera.   A quick aside: One interesting example of the what we wear category is sometimes called "white coat syndrome"—the main idea being that dogs come to form negative associations with vet's coats, which are white, and therefore experience increased distress levels when with a veterinarian (or other person) wearing a white coat. It's also interesting to consider the colors that dogs see best: Blue, and yellow. Outside of those, most of the colors humans see are variations of gray to dogs. Is it possible, then, that wearing certain colors can help or hinder our work with dogs? Or that the colors we choose for dogs' items, such as dog mats and toys, may be relevant? This seems a reasonable hypothesis.

CONTROLLABLE

There are many potential aversives within a handler's control. These might be either purposely or inadvertently delivered. A few examples of purposefully delivered aversives include withdrawal of access to a positive reinforcer such as attention, timeouts, verbal correction, noise correction, leash correction and other physical corrections, threatening or intimidating posture and behavior toward the dog, and electric corrections such as those found in remote collars, bark collars, and invisible fences.

Some aversives are delivered inadvertently. These are also under a handler's control, but the handler must first realize the presence of the inadvertent stimulus. Animal handlers can video their interactions to review them for these aversives.

Examples of inadvertent aversives include things like proximity, loud speech, eye contact, touch, or physical orientation with which the dog is uncomfortable such as hovering over, clicking or other startling reward marker (for noise phobic dogs), unconsidered use of collars, head harnesses, or other equipment uncomfortable for the dog; sudden, quick, or unusual movements, ending a training, play, or other enrichment session abruptly or injudiciously, forgetting to provide a reinforcer after desired behavior, et cetera. These are only a few examples of myriad possibilities, which is why it is so important to record oneself when working with a dog.

Note that one common trait in all three categories of aversives is the potential for causing or leveraging fear. This is important to be on guard against. And though this may seem paradoxical, it's also important to understand that "fear-free" isn't possible. After all, fear is a survival response that serves animals well; without it, there would be little to no animals, including humans. Since we do not get to decide what is aversive to a particular dog, and since fear is a natural survival mechanism, no one can be a completely "fear-free" handler.

What is possible, and crucial, is to do everything within our power to avoid causing new fears, and to refuse to leverage existing fears. Indeed, starting from this commitment can be a great way to begin the metamorphosis to anti-aversives. It is by commiting to an anti-aversives stance that we have the best chance of avoiding fear.

False Claims regarding Aversives

As we already know, anything that results in fear, pain, distress, or discomfort brings with it an increased risk of behavior problems and therefore an increased risk of death for the dog. Here are the most common false and confused claims regarding aversives:

FALSE: "Shock collars [and other aversives] save lives."

The nonsensical rationale for this one usually has to do with either the "last resort" claim for dogs presenting with undesired behavior—including aggression, fear, separation anxiety, and other conditions that are in reality treatable with an anti-aversives approach—or with fallacious claims related to recall and other obedience. The truth is that *positive* training saves lives because it inspires the dog to want to learn desired behavior and to want to pay attention to the handler; a good positive handler is one who knows how to become the most reinforcing thing in the dog's environment.

FALSE: "Since our mission is to save lives, we must use all training options 'in the toolbox' to address behavior problems and therefore avoid euthanasia."

Those using this argument need to realize that the argument is self-negating because the science shows that aversive training *leads* to behavior problems, which lead to euthanasia. If one truly wants to stick to a lifesaving mission, the wise choice is to stop doing things to dogs that cause them distress and ultimately put their lives at risk. Elective euthanasia performed a year or several later still means that life was not saved.

FALSE: "It doesn't hurt or scare them. It just gets their attention."

Aversives result in the human's desired effect ONLY by hurting, scaring, or otherwise discomforting the dog. One basic principle of aversives is that adding an unpleasant stimulus results in the reduction or elimination of an undesired behavior; another principle is that removal of an unpleasant stimulus only after the dog behaves as commanded results in an increase in the commanded behavior. If the shock, prong, or tightening collar, leash jerk, squirting, yelling, or other aversive stimulus "worked" in that moment, or if the cessation of an aversive stimulus "worked" in that moment, *by definition* this means it hurt, scared, or otherwise discomforted the dog. If a handler truly just wants to get a dog's attention, there are many humane ways, including the obvious and well-proven call or other cue, accomplished through the animal's positive associations with the cue.

CONFUSED: "There must be consequences for bad behavior."

This sort of comment often comes with an accusation regarding the ineffectiveness of "purely positive" training. Both comments show that the commenter doesn't understand operant and classical conditioning, nor the dynamics of training.

Operant conditioning, which positive reinforcement training is, is *based* on consequences. The dog executes a cued behavior and the consequence is that the dog gets paid with something the dog really enjoys – the reward is a consequence. If the dog does not execute the cued behavior, the dog does not get paid—the witholding of the coveted reward is a consequence. If non-execution of behavior continues to happen, a reputable trainer will acknowledge that the training process needs to be checked for things like mechanics and clarity as well as consider whether the training plan needs to be rewritten. In other words, instead of blaming the dog, labeling the dog or the behavior as hopeless or otherwise "bad" and therefore deciding that aversives are needed, the reputable trainer will adjust his own behavior.

The term "purely positive" is a straw man used to dishonestly or naively attempt to denigrate positive reinforcement. Educated trainers know that it is impossible to be "purely" positive just as it is impossible to completely avoid aversive experiences. But educated, reputable trainers also understand that this is no excuse to employ or condone aversives. The existence of rain, thunder, and lightning in the life of nature does not mean that things like squirting, shake cans, and shock collars should exist in the life of animals. The fact that nothing is perfect—"purely positive"—does not mean we should give up our morals and give in to aversives.

FALSE: "You need to add a punishment that is intolerable to the dog or else it won't work."

On one hand, this claim, stated by a well-known aversive trainer, proves that the aversive trainer knows that shock and other aversives do indeed hurt and frighten, and that they are intended to do so by their users. 'The plan is pain' is what this quote suggests. On the other hand, anyone who has ever trained or behavior-modified a dog without the use of aversives knows the statement's underlying belief that aversives are required is false. Thousands of modern trainers do not need to add any punishment, let alone extreme punishment implied by the term "intolerable," in order for training to work. Learning theory implies that both positive reinforcement and aversives 'work'—though in distinctly different ways and durations. Humane trainers choose the positive way, which does not condone causing or exacerbating suffering.

FALSE: "The aversive worked [e.g., the dog stopped pulling after being hit]; that's all that matters."

"Worked" here means the pulling stopped for that moment. But unless the dog never pulled again after that, the aversive didn't really work. It just hurt or scared the dog enough to stun-stop the dog temporarily, in that moment, not permanently.

Moreover, that something "works" is not all that matters. If effectiveness were all that mattered, abuse of animals and humans wouldn't be illegal as well as shameful and immoral. What also matters is the dog's associations and emotional condition, because an otherwise healthy dog who presents with undesired behavior is almost always a dog whose undesired behavior is informed by underlying emotions and negative associations.

FALSE: "Behavior modification is supposed to be hard."

Behavior modification might be boring for some handlers. It sometimes is slow due to the methodical nature of humane work. But it isn't supposed to be hard. For the dog it can be hard if the practitioner employs aversives or worse yet is blatantly abusive, but it isn't *supposed* to be hard. On the contrary, it's supposed to be safe, humane, and achievable. For the trainer it's only hard if that trainer's temperament or education are a bad match for performing behavior modification—for example if the practicioner is impatient or has not had access to obtaining the appropriate skills.

FALSE: "Behavior modification isn't pretty"

Actually, behavior modification done well—that is, anti-aversively—is a beautiful thing. Those who know how to do this, know this.

The potential for negative consequences when one uses aversives are many, including:

Learned Helplessness: Animals who are repeatedly confronted with aversive stimuli over which they have no control or ability to avoid may develop the sense that escape and avoidance are impossible, resulting in a lasting inertia or "general shutdown." This condition, especially when held long-term, may result in the generalized suppression of behavior *overall*, as the result of habitual forced suppression. Unfortunately, such passive animals are sometimes prized for being "easy-to-live-with" or mistaken for animals with angelic temperaments, their suffering unrecognized. An example of this might be an animal who is confined to her crate most of every day and night, such as a racetrack dog or a lab animal who, upon release and homing, appears to be an easy-going "couch potato" or who tolerates situations, without reaction, that the average dog could not.

Aggression & Reactivity: Some animals being hurt or scared by a handler may attempt to protect themselves by displaying ritualized aggression to the handler—that is, behavior intended to scare the aggressor (the aversives-deliverer) away in order to avoid actual aggression. This is known as distance-increasing behavior, and often generalizes to others the animal associates with the handler or the aversive, such as other people, other animals, or any other stimuli—including treats—that were present at the time of the aversive delivery or that appears similar to the aversive deliverer. Once in a while, ritualized aggression may morph into a bite, whether out of growing distress, panic, or because there is truly no other way the animal can self-defend; that is, the animal finds that the only way to protect herself is to defend herself from the deliverer of the aversive, which by now is himself an aversive to this animal.

Redirection: An animal in a highly aversive situation may also present with aggressive—that is, self-defensive—responses to others in the vicinity who were not involved, in what may be argued is an involuntary response. The highly distressed animal goes into survival mode and usual cognitive function is thereby hindered, replaced by the instinct to survive and the behaviors that support survival.

Anxiety: An animal who experiences aversives regularly may develop anxiety—a consistent feeling that something bad is going to happen—and the nervous or reactive behaviors that result from living in a state of anxiety.

Fear: A very common if not inevitable result of aversives is that the animal becomes afraid not only of the aversive and possibly anything similar to it, but also of the deliverer of the aversive, any other stimuli that were present at the time of the delivery of the aversive, and contexts similar to the one in which the aversive was delivered. In other words, the animal may develop sensitivities to various conditions associated with the aversive experiences, leading to a tendency to startle and/ or attempts to avoid or escape, e.g., to dart away, which can be dangerous or fatal.

Avoidance & Escape: As a result of the developed anxiety or fear, the animal may also become habitually avoidant, or may develop and employ escape behavior whenever an opportunity presents itself.

Landmining: This is my own term, though

the commonly used term "fallout" is related. Landmining refers to the fact that temporary suppression, especially if suppression is repeated consistently, of an undesired behavior bears with it the risk of that or similar undesired behavior resurfacing unexpectedly or explosively. The many cases of dogs treated with shock collars to try to resolve biting, for example, who down the road present with much more damaging bites are examples of this. Oftentimes these resurfaced bite behaviors come seemingly without warning, because aversives were used to suppress *all* behavior considered undesirable: barking, growling, snarling, et cetera. It is not yet common knowledge outside the professional canine behavior world that suppressing a dog's growl, for example,—which is a dog's way of letting you know "I'm not comfortable with this; please stop it"—increases the chance of a bite that seems unprovoked or "out of nowhere." In reality, such a dog was trained to suppress his means of communication so is more likely to take an action like a bite without first giving an obvious indicator of what is coming if provocation continues. Growls and other communication provide us with information that are opportunities to prevent a bite by changing our own behavior and/or other antecedents in the environment.

Generalization of ritualized aggression, self-defense responses, escape, or avoidance behaviors to additional contexts.

Learning Difficulties & Health Problems: The increased biochemical stress levels of animals living with aversives may lead to a variety of medical problems and cognitive difficulties.

Injuries and Fatalities: When an aversive is used on an animal, there is a risk of physical injury as well as emotional injury, not only directly—as when a tightened collar collapses a trachea or results in eye prolapse—but also indirectly, as when an animal trying to avoid something aversive darts in front of a moving car or falls down a staircase.

Escalation by the Deliverer: When a person uses aversives on an animal, that person is reinforced for the use of the aversive every time it "works" even temporarily. A principle of operant learning theory teaches us the result on the person: That person will tend to repeat or increase the use of aversives since the person has been reinforced for doing so. Then, when the aversive or level of aversive in use stops working as the dog habituates to it, the person, in what may be compared to an extinction burst, will increase the intensity of the aversive, or employ a more painful or frightening aversive, until he gets the result he demands. In other words, the risks of cruelty are increased.

Consequences of Anti-Aversives

When we talk about consequences of training and behavior choices made for our dogs, often the focus is on negative consequences, which is understandable and fair. But it's also important to talk about the positive consequences of an anti-aversives stance. Below are just a few of these consequences:

Enjoyable Training and Handling: Anti-aversive dog training is more fun. Very few people would say they find it fun to hurt, intimidate, or scare their dogs. Furthermore, dogs trained anti-aversively are more enjoyable to handle because they know that the consequences of their behavior will be something they want rather than something they fear. As a result, they are very enthusiastic about training.

Mutual, Positive, Reinforcement: **R+ works to increase desired behavior by providing something desireable to the animal as a reward for the animal having executed the behavior desired by the handler. The dog comes to understand that the paycheck (reward) is earned by repeating the behavior the handler desires. At the same time, the handler finds that the more the dog is paid (rewarded) for executing the handler's desired behavior, the more likely, and more easily, the dog will continue to behave as desired. Therefore, both dog and handler build strong, consistent habits of behaving in ways that access the reinforcement (the reward) each wants, and thus they continue to add to one another's lives in ways that create and maintain happiness.

Happiness and Enthusiasm: Dogs anti-aversively, R+ trained are more enthusiastic during training sessions and more enthusiastic in regard to their handlers in general because a strong history of positive reinforcement has been built and is now trusted. Of course, dogs who are enthusiastic about behavior as requested by their handlers add happiness to their handlers' lives. Of interest: At least one study suggests that dogs trained anti-aversively by their owners *play* more in the presence of their owners.

Quick and Stable Learning: Anti-aversive training is more stable, more easily understood by the animal, and the learning more reliably retained, because of the clear, timely connection made between the desired behavior and the reward and because of the positive associations created during the process. Naturally, such a dog has a reduced risk of anxiety, which means an increased likelihood of behavioral stability.

Respects the Self and Others and Encourages Cognitive Strength: As members of a culture that believes in civility, self-respect and respect from others are positively reinforcing. When we respect others, especially those whom we care about such as our dogs, our intellectual vigor is thereby also reinforced, rather than hindered by unconscious or conscious guilt, shame, frustration, and other negative feelings. An anti-aversive lifestyle is a lifestyle based in respect and cognitive vigor. Furthermore, studies suggest that animals may achieve positive affective states as a result of their own achievements, and since anti-aversive learning leads to more achievement for an animal, cognition may be positively impacted.

Lasting, Resilient Bonds Built on a Solid Foundation of Tenderness and Trust: It seems logical that tenderness with an animal, whether human or non-human, positively impacts the trust that animal develops in the tender person. Equally logical is that trust and tenderness help build and maintain resilient bonds between the parties. The science also supports these ideas. One study, for example, concludes that the bonding of the dog to the owner is not only more consistent in dogs trained with reward-based training, but also that aversive-based training is related to a *lack* of bond.

Reduction of Cultural Heartache: When we mistreat the animals we claim to adore, whom we believe are our "best friends," we psychologically harm ourselves as well as them. This dual harm quickly becomes, has become, a vicious cycle. But it can stop and we can be better.

It can be easy to blame "human nature" for our self-centered behavior—behavior that too often includes neglect, abandonment, or abuse. But as cultural psychologist Dr. Steven Heine says, human nature is not an innate, fixed thing:

> *[H]uman nature is not something that's inside us. Humans come into this world ready to acquire our natures....*

*Human nature is about learning
from our experiences and having
those experiences become part of us.*

Currently, the experiences that have become part of us—that have created our "nature" to date—include our stories and how we tell them, based on our beliefs that our companion animals are beloved by us, and yet contradicted by the fact that somewhere between 6 and 8 million of our companion animals lose their homes with us every year, being brought to shelters instead. This is just one way in which our culture is a culture of cognitive dissonance and, as a result, psychological suffering. Cultural heartache.

Cultural psychologist Dr. Marianna Pogosyan says that "culture leaves an undeniable imprint on our emotional narratives, including the way we feel and think of distress, how it manifests and how we cope with it." How do we currently cope with the contradictions we manifest regarding our companion animals? We minimize. We rationalize. We deny. We reject. We intend to do better next time. We grieve. We grieve. We are full of grief.

Our culture grief also manifests more denial. We dismiss the distress and grief of others as "compassion fatigue." That begins the cycle again.

To heal our cultural heartache, we must make major changes, building muscles strong enough to stop the cycles of suffering. Per Dr. Yulia Chentsova-Dutton, depression tends to revolve around loss, with traumatic events as risk factors. Surrendering a dog to a shelter is a traumatic event for many people. Deciding to euthanize is a traumatic event for most people. Chentsova-Dutton explains that in the west, we try to distance ourselves from our distress by attributing it to biomedical causes—to "essentialize depression" as a characteristic of our biology, but that this backfires because it encourages us to ignore other factors influencing our sadness.

She also points to social stability and functional relationships as two protective factors against depression. Many of us consider our relationships with our companion animals among the most stable, important relationships we have. How do we square that with the devastation our companion animals endure? Can a community, a culture, a society, that loves its pets so deeply continue to accept their less than stellar station without traumatizing itself as well? No. It is impossible.

Heal the plight of our beloved companions, heal ourselves.

**Note: From my perspective, if a person uses aversive forms of training in addition to R+ (positive reinforcement) on a dog, it is inaccurate to say that the person is training via positive reinforcement because once an aversive is added, positive reinforcement is negated. To say otherwise would be like saying that a regularly beaten child was raised by positive reinforcement simply because that child also was rewarded with cookies sometimes.

Achieving an Anti-Aversives Culture

This may sound daunting, but in many ways it is simple. Advocate for our animals—with trainers and behavior consultants. —in the veterinary office. —at the groomer's. —at the boarder's. —with dog sitters and dog walkers. —with family, friends, and colleagues. Everywhere we take, or do not take, a dog is an opportunity to improve advocacy for them.

Keep them safe. Aversives can make our companions unsafe. But there are myriad other threats to their safety. Consider every action and situation before exposing the dog. Some things cannot be undone so must be avoided. Advocacy with others is part of keeping them safe; advocacy within ourselves helps us make the best decisions and take the safest actions for our dogs.

Keep them *feeling* safe. Aversives make our dogs feel unsafe. In a way, we may define an aversive as anything that makes the dog feel unsafe; to feel unsafe is an aversive condition. Is the dog afraid of walks? Help her feel safe by not insisting on a walk; find another means of enrichment until she can be anti-aversively reconditioned regarding walks. Is the dog afraid of people? Protect her from aversive exposure—too close, too intense, too long—to people until she can be anti-aversively reconditioned regarding people. An anti-aversive stance is a stance that helps the dog feel safe.

Reject obsolete premises and practices. Family may say "it's just a dog" but we know the dog is a creature who contains multitudes—emotions, memories, intelligence, affection, and more. Let our rejection of obsolete beliefs be a start to showing others the reality. Friends may chide us for "coddling" rather than "disciplining" but anyone who has ever had a friend help them feel better via any sort of coddling behavior knows how helpful such support and reassurance can be. On the other hand, anyone who has ever been disciplined knows the hurt feelings and damage it can cause. Keep in mind, too, that a human disciplining another human has the benefit of explaining the rationale for such action. This is a not a benefit available for our companion animals; if we discipline them, they only know the fear, distress, or pain. As far as we know, they may not even comprehend that the fear, distress, and pain of an act of discipline will end—nor that doesn't represent a threat of death.

Promote responsibility and take responsibility. Lifesaving does not complete at point of sale; it threads through treatment, training, placement, ongoing follow-up, and lifelong support and protection. We are responsible, forever, for all whom we have tamed. *We* are.

Replace current presumptions and habits with innovative improvements to achieve safety and well-being. Commit to an anti-aversives lifestyle. Implement a training & behavior literacy (TBL) program for the caregivers of all animals for whom we were, and therefore are, responsible—the animals to whom we have made an implicit promise, whether by buying, adopting, rescuing, or homing them. Proudly speak of these commitments, promises, and new habits to others. Behave as if they are the norm until they become the norm.

Implement thought, communication, and action that increases companion animal safety and well-being. At the same time, continue to encourage, support, and inspire others to do the same.

In other words: Become at once a beacon and a guidebook. You have it within you.

All the suffering in the world
are distortions of our ability to love.
How then are we to love?
With tenderness. Without passion.
Every time our judgment is clouded
by the ardent passions that consume us,
we give love a dangerous concreteness....
In short, we are causing pain—
to ourselves and to others.
Replace that concrete love with tenderness.

"The New Pope"

REFERENCES

Azrin, N. H., & Holz, W. C. (1966). "Punishment" in W. K. Honig (Ed.), *Operant Behavior: Areas of Research and Application.* New York: Appleton-Century-Crofts.

Bihm, Elson M.; J. Arthur Gillaspy, Jr. (2012). "Marian Breland Bailey (1920–2001)". *The Encyclopedia of Arkansas History & Culture.* The Central Arkansas Library System.

Cambridge Center for Behavioral Studies. https://behavior.org/help-centers/animal-behavior/companion-animals/ Retrieved 2/1/2020

Chance, P. *Learning and Behavior.* Wadsworth, 2002

Coren, S. "Do Dogs Actually Use Color Vision?" (2013) Psychology Today. https://www.psychologytoday.com/us/blog/canine-corner/201307/do-dogs-actually-use-color-vision Retrieved 2/2/2010

Grohmann, K., et al. (2013) "Severe Brain Damage after Putative Training Technique..." *Journal of Veterinary Behavior*

Donaldson, J. *The Culture Clash.* Tantor, 2017

Estes, William K., & Skinner, B.F. (1941) "Some quantitative properties of anxiety." *Journal of Experimental Psychology* Vol 29

Evans, E.P. *The Criminal Prosecution and Capital Punishment of Animals* London, 1906

FDA Compliance Enforcement https://www.fda.gov/regulatory-information/search-fda-guidance-documents/cpg-sec-655300-barking-dog-collar retrieved 1/30/2020

Fearful Dogs Project, The. www.fearfuldogsproject.org

Fernando III, A. & Consedine, NS. (2014) "Beyond compassion fatigue: the transactional model of physician compassion". *Journal of Pain and Symptom Management.* Vol 48

Fernando III, A. (2016) "Enhancing compassion in general practice: it's not all about the doctor." *British Journal of General Practice.* Vol 66

Friedman, Susan G. "What's Wrong with This Picture? Effectiveness is not Enough." *APDT Journal.* March/April 2010

Hammerle, M., et al. (2015) "AAHA Canine and Feline Behavior Management Guidelines." *Journal of the American Animal Hospital Association.* Vol 51

Herron, M., Shofer, F., & Reisner, I. (2009) "Survey of the use and outcome of confrontational and non-confrontational training methods in client-owned dogs showing undesired behaviors." *Applied Animal Behavior Science* Vol 117

Humane Society of the United States, *Animal Rescue Shelters in the US industry trends* (2014-2019) https://www.ibisworld.com/united-states/market-research-reports/animal-rescue-shelters-industry/ retrieved 2/20/2020

Koehler, W. *The Koehler Method of Dog Training.* Howell Book House, 1962.

Maier, S. F., & Seligman, M.E. (1976) "Learned helplessness: Theory and evidence." *Journal of Experimental Psychology*

McGowan, R., et al. "Positive affect and learning: exploring the "Eureka Effect" in dogs" (2014) *Animal Cognition* Vol 17

Mead, Margaret as quoted by her institute, The Institute for Inteculture Studies. http://interculturalstudies.org/Mead/index.html retrieved 2/5/2020

Pogosyan, Marianna. "Insights into Human Nature from Cultural Psychology" (2019) *Psychology Today* https://www.psychologytoday.com/us/blog/between-cultures/201905/insights-human-nature-cultural-psychology retrieved 2/2/2020

Ibid. "How Culture Affects Depression" (2017) *Psychology Today* https://www.psychologytoday.com/us/blog/between-cultures/201712/how-culture-affects-depression retrieved 2/2/2020.

Powell, R.A., Honey, P.L, & Symbaluk, D.G. *Introduction to Learning and Behavior.* Cengage Learning, 2016

Protect Them All. www.protectthemall.org

Saunders, Blanche as referred to in *Training You to Train Your Dog* (1954) Periscope Film. Video https://www.youtube.com/watch?v=JQlpypAfULs&list=WL&index=2&t=0s retrieved 2/2/2020

Schalke, E., et al. (2007) "Clinical Signs Caused by the Use of Electric Training Collars on Dogs in Everyday Life Situations." *Applied Animal Behaviour Science* Vol 105

Scully, Matthew. *Dominion: The Power of Man, the Suffering of Animals, and the Call to Mercy.* St. Martins Griffin, 2002

Sulzer-Azaroff, Beth, & Mayer, G. Roy. *Behavior Analysis for Lasting Change*. Wadsworth, 1991

Vieira de Castro, A., et al "Carrots versus sticks: The Relationship between Training Methods and Dog-owner Attachment" (2019) *Applied Animal Behaviour Science*, Vol 219

Winograd, N., *Redemption* (2014) Sagacity Productions.

Ziv, Gal. "The Effects of Using Aversive Training Methods in Dogs." (2017) *Journal of Veterinary Behavior*. Vol 19.